CW00970726

# Shaking Hands
# with Death

www.**terrypratchett**.co.uk

# Shaking Hands with Death

Terry Pratchett

**CORGI BOOKS**

TRANSWORLD PUBLISHERS
61–63 Uxbridge Road, London W5 5SA
www.transworldbooks.co.uk

Transworld is part of the Penguin Random House group of companies
whose addresses can be found at global.penguinrandomhouse.com

First broadcast on BBC1 in 2010 as The Richard Dimbleby Lecture
First published in *A Slip of the Keyboard* by Doubleday in 2014
This edition first published in Great Britain
in 2015 by Corgi Books
an imprint of Transworld Publishers

A CIP catalogue record for this book
is available from the British Library.

ISBN
9780552172776

Typeset in 12/16pt Adobe Caslon by Falcon Oast Graphic Art Ltd.
Printed and bound by Clays Ltd, Bungay, Suffolk.

Penguin Random House is committed to a sustainable
future for our business, our readers and our planet. This book is made
from Forest Stewardship Council® certified paper.

3 5 7 9 10 8 6 4 2

# Shaking Hands
# with Death

## Introduction
## by Rob Wilkins

In the autumn of 2009 Terry was approached by the Dimbleby family about the possibility of his delivering the annual televised lecture inaugurated by them four decades ago in memory of Richard Dimbleby. At that time, Terry was filled with a white-hot rage at being diagnosed with a rare form of Alzheimer's disease at the ridiculously young age of fifty-nine, and at the lack of choice available to people in his position over how and when to end their suffering. He accepted, and began to write.

Working his way through the first draft of

*Shaking Hands with Death* channelled Terry's fury into something positive: the fury became his inspiration. But Terry was doubtful that what he was writing would actually make it on to television; he was convinced that the BBC would never agree to broadcast a lecture on the subject of death and dying, and the difficulties we have to endure towards the end of our lives. Despite this, instead of tempering his anger, Terry wound up his fury to eleven and pressed on regardless.

Terry had lost the ability to touch-type by this point – one of the first casualties of the war against his disease – and so he dictated the early drafts of the lecture directly to his computer. We had trained the dictation program, TalkingPoint, to understand Terry's voice and recognize all the unique names and places in his novels; he was overjoyed that it rattled past a Weatherwax and a Vetinari, and secretly thrilled when it stumbled over simple words such as 'pioneer' (which it delightfully transcribed as 'pie on ear'). However, the anger in his voice as he tried to line up his thoughts about what he saw as the misery of end-of-life care was unmistakable, and the software just couldn't cope with the change of tone. Try as he might to get his words on to the page, Terry was unable to express his passion without bellowing the words, so I stepped in and let him shout at me on the keyboard instead.

We first presented what was essentially the text you have here to a kindly BBC producer over cappuccinos in the café of the National Theatre. While Terry sipped his frothy coffee, the BBC executive read all the way through to the end without stopping, his expression unreadable. And then there was a long pause, followed by a huge smile, and I realized that the BBC were going to allow this lecture after all. Terry had managed his anger in exactly the right way – using it to explore unflinchingly how society is going to have to redefine death in an increasingly elderly population; and he had done so in a sympathetic and human way. Anyone who has read one of Terry's novels will know how he could spin the most beautiful sentences and make his craft look effortless – it was what made him such a huge success. Now he was using that talent not for another wonderful piece of fiction, not for his own benefit at all, but to deal with a very real issue that we are all, at some point in our futures, going to have to face.

On the morning of 1 February 2010, we arrived at the Royal College of Physicians, the venue for the lecture, to find film crews already waiting on the pavement outside. Interest in what Terry was going to say was mounting. A tense moment followed as rival networks battled for their lunchtime exclusives, but Terry – in his customary gentlemanly way – spoke to each of them in turn and gave them all something unique.

Terry was due to speak in the college's magnificent library – appropriately, since he was the first novelist to give a Dimbleby Lecture. The library's oak-panelled walls were lined with dusty old leather tomes, secured behind iron bars. There seemed something poignant about this, all those words kept behind lock and key so they couldn't escape and speak for themselves – and here amongst them was Terry, his lecture rolled nonchalantly in his hands. I knew how much effort it had cost him to get those words down on paper.

Now, though, came the next challenge, as the cameras got ready to roll for the first rehearsal. This moment had been causing me great concern. Recently Terry had been finding reading a particular struggle, even when he used hugely enlarged fonts spread across the bank of computer screens in our office. How was he going to deal with auto-cues and their continuously scrolling type?

Thankfully, Terry had been pondering his enforced limitations too, and he came up with a solution; he suggested – to my delight but trepidation – that I should read the lecture for him. The BBC agreed so long as he was able to give an introduction, and so we hastily tapped out something suitable. I had spoken for Terry on many occasions before and was soon to read from his latest novel at a packed Sydney Opera House, but this time there was much more at stake. The opportunity to give a Dimbleby Lecture was a once-in-a-lifetime chance – and Terry's hard-won words were so important. Would a 'stunt Pratchett', as Terry termed it, work? We took to the stage. Terry gave his introduction flawlessly and I read the rest of his words with the passion

I had heard him put into them during his long hours of writing. There was enough backslapping afterwards for us to realize that this 'stunt Pratchett' approach had worked – Terry's words carried weight even when it was not his voice speaking them. And there were still more than six hours left to work on the performance. The lecture was on track.

As it happened, Tony Robinson – a good friend of Terry's – was at that moment flying back into the country to join us for the lecture. We had emailed Terry's text to him and he read it on a tiny screen in the back of a bumpy taxi ride from Heathrow into central London. When Tony arrived at the library for tea and a catch-up, the producer suggested he read the lecture on stage and give me some pointers. In front of a lighting rig and cameras, Tony read *Shaking Hands with Death*. It was a masterclass in public speaking. All of the emotion that had driven Terry on to write was delivered with absolute clarity into the hearts of everyone listening. It was clear to us all that this was how Terry's lecture should be heard, and so, when the cameras rolled that evening, Terry delivered his powerful opening paragraphs to a rapt audience and handed over to Tony to read the rest.

The lecture was recorded as 'live' early in the evening, and by the time it was broadcast to the nation a little later, we were all enjoying a celebratory dinner. It achieved everything Terry could have hoped for. Mr Alzheimer's didn't become Dr Death – as he had feared he would – overnight, but the subject matter had touched the TV audience and was starting meaningful debate. Terry never thought that his lecture would or could change the draconian UK end-of-life laws, but he managed to get the public and the politicians talking. It was for this that he had harnessed his anger and overcome the challenge of getting the lecture out of his head and on to the page and television screen. He was to keep that conversation and that debate going for years to come, and continued to campaign no matter how difficult his illness made it, on the subject that mattered so much to him.

Terry finally shook hands with Death on 12 March 2015. His was a peaceful end, surrounded by his family, and with Pongo – his beloved tabby cat – dutifully sleeping at the foot of his bed. He didn't want unnecessary care, he didn't want tubes and pipes keeping him alive; he wanted all of us to have the option of dying with dignity at a time of our own choosing. And whether you share Terry's views and opinions or not, there is no doubt that his was a life well lived.

RW
June 2015

# Shaking Hands
with Death

Broadcast on BBC1 on 1 February 2010
from the Royal Society of Medicine

Firstly I must express my gratitude and grateful thanks to the Dimbleby family for asking me to give this lecture today.

I cherish what I suspect is at least part of their reason for inviting me. I was a young newspaper journalist, still learning his trade, when Richard Dimbleby died of cancer in late December 1965. Two pieces of information shook the nation: one was that he had died and the other was that his family said that he had died of cancer. At that time it was the disease whose name was unspoken. People died of 'a long illness' and as journalists we accepted and connived at this furtive terminology. However, we all knew what it

19

meant, yet nobody used the forbidden word. But overnight, people were talking about this, and as a result it seemed to me the war on cancer began in earnest. Before you can kill the monster you have to say its name.

It was the distant echo of that example that prompted me to stand up two years ago and reveal that I had a form of Alzheimer's disease. I remembered the shameful despairing way cancer had been hidden in darkness. That and the Dimbleby family's decision to be open about Richard's death were at the soul and centre of my own decision, which I made because of the sheer impossibility of not doing so. It was not a decision, in fact. It was a determination and a reckoning.

My name is Terry Pratchett and I am the author of a very large number of inexplicably popular fantasy novels.

Contrary to popular belief, fantasy is not

about making things up. The world is stuffed full of things. It is almost impossible to invent any more. No, the role of fantasy as defined by G. K. Chesterton is to take what is normal and everyday and usual and unregarded, and turn it around and show it to the audience from a different direction, so that they look at it once again with new eyes.

I intend tonight to talk about Alzheimer's disease, which I am glad to say is no longer in the twilight, but also about another once taboo subject, the nature of our relationship with death.

Regrettably I have to point out that the nature of my disease may not allow me to read all the way through this lecture. If this is the case, we have arranged for my friend Tony Robinson, who made a very moving programme about his own mother's struggle with dementia, to step in and be your stunt Terry Pratchett for the evening.

I'm sure you know that, for my sins, which I wish I could remember because they must have been crimson, I am effectively 'Mr Alzheimer's' and I have given more interviews on the subject than I can remember. But there are others, less well known, who have various forms of dementia and go out and about being ambassadors for the Alzheimer's Society in their fight against the wretched disease. It's not just me, by a long way. They are unsung heroes and I salute them.

When I was a young boy, playing on the floor of my grandmother's front room, I glanced up at the television and saw Death, talking to a Knight, and I didn't know very much about death at that point. It was the thing that happened to budgerigars and hamsters. But it was Death, with a scythe and an amiable manner. I didn't know it at the time, of course, but I had just watched a clip from Bergman's *Seventh Seal*, wherein the Knight engages in protracted dialogue, and of course the famous chess game, with the Grim Reaper who, it seemed to me, did not seem so terribly grim.

The image has remained with me ever since and Death as a character appeared in the very first of my Discworld novels. He has evolved in the series to be one of its most popular characters; implacable, because that is his job, he nevertheless appears to have some sneaking regard and compassion for a race of creatures which are to him as ephemeral as mayflies, but which nevertheless spend their brief lives making rules for the universe and counting the stars. He is, in short, a kindly Death, cleaning up the mess that this life leaves, and opening the gate to the next one. Indeed, in some religions he is an angel.

People have written to me about him from convents, ecclesiastical palaces, funeral parlours and, not least, hospices. The letters I've had from people all around the world have sometimes made me give up writing for the day and take a long walk. It is touching, and possibly worrying that people will write, with some difficulty, a six-page letter to an author they have never met, and include in it sentiments that I very much doubt they would share with their doctor.

I have no clear recollection of the death of my grandparents, but my paternal grandfather died in the ambulance on the way to hospital just after having cooked and eaten his own dinner at the age of ninety-six. (It turned out, when we found his birth certificate, that he was really ninety-four, but he was proud of being ninety-six, so I hope that no celestial being was kind enough to disillusion him.)

He had felt very odd, got a neighbour to ring for the doctor and stepped tidily into the ambulance and out of the world. He died on the way to the hospital – a good death if ever there was one. Except that, according to my father, he did complain to the ambulance men that he hadn't had time to finish his pudding. I am not at all sure about the truth of this, because my father had a finely tuned sense of humour which he was good enough to bequeath to me, presumably to make up for the weak bladder, the short stature and the male-pattern baldness, which regrettably came with the package.

My father's own death was more pro-tracted. He had a year's warning. It was pancreatic cancer. Technology kept him alive, at home and in a state of reasonable comfort and cheerfulness for that year, during which we had those conversations that you have with a dying parent. Perhaps it is when you truly get to know them, when you realize that it is now you marching towards the sound of the guns and you are ready to listen to the

advice and reminiscences that life was too
crowded for up to that point. He unloaded
all the anecdotes that I had heard before,
about his time in India during the war, and
came up with a few more that I had never
heard. As with so many men of his generation, his wartime service was never far from
his recollection. Then, at one point, he suddenly looked up and said, 'I can feel the sun
of India on my face,' and his face did light
up rather magically, brighter and happier
than I had seen it at any time in the previous
year and if there had been any justice or even
narrative sensibility in the universe, he would
have died there and then, shading his eyes
from the sun of Karachi.

He did not.

On the day he was diagnosed my father
told me, and I quote: 'If you ever see me in
a hospital bed, full of tubes and pipes and no
good to anybody, tell them to switch me off.'

In fact, it took something under a fortnight in the hospice for him to die as a kind of collateral damage in the war between his cancer and the morphine. And in that time he stopped being him and started becoming a corpse, albeit one that moved ever so slightly from time to time.

There wasn't much I could have done, and since the nurses in the Welsh hospice were fine big girls, perhaps that was just as well. I thank them now for the geriatric cat that was allowed to roam the wards and kept me and my mother company as we awaited the outcome. Feline though it was, and also slightly smelly, with a tendency to grumble, it was a touch of humanity in the long reaches of the night.

On the way back home after my father's death I scraped my Jag along a stone wall in Hay-on-Wye. To be fair, it's almost impossible not to scrape Jags along the walls in

Hay-on-Wye even if your eyes aren't clouded with tears, but what I didn't know at the time, yet strongly suspect now, was that also playing a part in that little accident was my own disease, subtly making its presence felt. Alzheimer's creeps up very gently over a long period of time, possibly decades, and Baby Boomers like myself know that we are never going to die so always have an explanation ready for life's little hiccups. We say, 'I've had a senior moment. Ha! Ha!' We say, 'Everybody loses their car keys.' We say, 'Oh, I do that, too. I often go upstairs and forget what I have come up for!' We say, 'I often forget someone's name mid sentence,' and thus we are complicit in one another's determination not to be mortal. We like to believe that if all of us are growing old, none of us are growing old.

I have touch-typed since I was thirteen, but now that was going wrong. I got new spectacles. I bought a better keyboard – not such a bad idea since the old one was full of beard hairs and coffee – and finally at the end of self-delusion I went to see my GP. Slightly apologetically she gave me the standard Alzheimer's test, with such taxing questions as 'What day of the week is it?' and then sent me off locally for a scan. The result? I didn't have Alzheimer's. My condition was simply wear and tear on the brain caused by the passage of time that 'happens to everybody'. Old age, in short. I thought, well, I've never been fifty-nine before and so this must be how it is.

So off I went, reassured, about my business; I did a signing tour in Russia, a signing tour in the USA, which included breakfast at the White House (there were lots of other people there, it wasn't as if I handed Mrs Bush the cornflakes or anything), and then I did a signing tour in Italy, where the wife of our ambassador very diplomatically pointed out that I had made a fist of buttoning up my shirt. Well, I had got up early for the flight, and had dressed in the dark, and so we all had a little chuckle, followed by lunch, and I hoped that everyone but me forgot about it.

Back home my typing was now so full of mistakes that it was simpler for me to dictate to my personal assistant. I went to see my GP again and she sent me to Addenbrooke's Hospital in Cambridge. I have never discussed the interview with her, but either by luck or prescience I ended up in front of Dr Peter Nestor, one of the few specialists in the country, or maybe the world, who would recognize Posterior Cortical Atrophy, the rare variant of my disease. He and his colleagues put me through a battery of tests, and he looked again at my scans, this time, importantly, in a different place. When he gave me the news that I had a rare form of Alzheimer's disease I quite genuinely saw him outlined in a rectangle of flaming red lines. We had a little bit of a discussion, and then, because the facility was closing for the day, I went home, passing another doctor putting on his bicycle clips – this was Cambridge, after all – and such was my state of mind that he too was outlined in red fire. The whole world had changed.

I was lucky in several ways. PCA is sufficiently different from 'classic' Alzheimer's that I have met fellow sufferers who dislike it being linked with that disease, even though the pathology and the endgame are ultimately the same. The journey, however, is different. PCA manifests itself through sight problems, and difficulty with topological tasks, such as buttoning up a shirt. I have the opposite of a superpower; sometimes, I cannot see what is there. I see the teacup with my eyes, but my brain refuses to send me the teacup message. It's very Zen. First there is no teacup and then, because I know there is a teacup, the teacup will appear the next time I look. I have little workarounds to deal with this sort of thing – people with PCA live in a world of workarounds. A glass revolving door is a potential Waterloo; I have a workaround for that now, too. In short, if you did not know there was anything wrong with me, you would not know there is anything wrong with me. People who have spoken to me for half an hour or so ask me if I am sure I have the illness. Yes, it's certainly there, but cunning and subterfuge get me through. So does money. The first draft of this speech was dictated using TalkingPoint on my computer which, while not perfect, produces a result that is marvellously better than anything I could tap out on the keyboard. From the inside, the disease makes me believe that I am constantly being followed by an invisible moron who moves things, steals things, hides things that I have put down a second before and, in general, sometimes causes me to yell with frustration. You see, the disease moves slowly, but you know it's there. Imagine that you're in a very, very slow motion car crash. Nothing much seems to be happening. There's an occasional little bang, a crunch, a screw pops out and spins across the dashboard as if we're in Apollo 13. But the radio is still playing, the heater is on and it doesn't seem all that bad, except for the certain knowledge that sooner or later you will be definitely going head first through the windscreen.

My first call when I got back from Cambridge was to my GP. I wanted to know what was going to happen next. In fact, it became clear that nothing at all was going to happen next unless we made it happen; there was no specialist anywhere local to me prepared to take on an early onset patient with PCA, and therefore nobody who could legitimately write me a prescription for the only palliative Alzheimer's drug on the market. When I learned this I was filled with a rage, a rage that is with me still, but by now tempered and harnessed to practical purposes. I felt alone. A cancer sufferer, just diagnosed, can at least have some map showing the way the future might, hopefully, go. And I don't seek to minimize how dreadful that disease would be, but there would be appointments, there would be specialists, there would be tests. Hopefully, you would receive sympathy, and hopefully you would have hope.

But at that time the Alzheimer's patient was more or less told to go home. Indeed, I have been contacted by patients who were in effect told just that, with not even the suggestion that they might talk to, for example, the Alzheimer's Society. I will say in another aside, I'm not the sort of person who goes to groups, but much later, I was persuaded to go to a PCA meeting in London, hosted by Professor Rosser of the National Hospital for Neurology and Neurosurgery. I remember the smiles when I started talking about the symptoms and it was hugely refreshing to be among people who understood without having to be told. But I had seen the bicycle clips of fire; I would have thrown a brick through a pharmacy window late at night for the medication I needed, and come to think of it, that might have made a damn good photo opportunity, but friends and contacts of mine who cared about my liberty helped me deal with the situation in the way that people deal with such situations in stupid hidebound bureaucracies. We bent things, just a tiny little bit. It wasn't as though I was stealing. I still had to pay for the damn drugs.

But then it was time to decide who I was

going to tell, and for the reasons given earlier, I decided to tell everybody. After that, my life ceased to be my own. I have had so much mail that not all of it can be answered in my lifetime. And I cannot remember how many interviews I have given. They must run into three figures easily. We did the BAFTA Award-winning documentary, in which I demonstrated to the world the impossibility of my tying a tie (funnily enough, I can tie my shoe laces, presumably because I have known how to do that for longer). I have also been able to write two more books, which my PA insists I tell you were bestsellers, had a stone bridge built over the stream in my garden, have been kissed by Joanna Lumley, and after being, astonishingly, knighted, subsequently made, with the help of knowledgeable friends, a sword – doing it the hard way, by first digging the iron ore out of the ground and smelting it in the garden. Of course, I shall never be able to take it out on the street, because such is the decay of our society that not even Knights can carry their swords in public. But who could ask for anything more? Except for, maybe, another kiss from Joanna Lumley.

But most of all in the last couple of years I have been listening. As a journalist, I learned to listen. It is amazing how much people will tell you if you listen in the right way. Rob, my PA, says that I can listen like a vacuum cleaner. Always beware of somebody who is a really good listener.

I have heard it said that some people feel that they are being avoided once the news gets around that they have Alzheimer's. For me it has been just the reverse. People want to talk to me, on city streets, in theatre queues, on aeroplanes over the Atlantic, even on country walks. They want to tell me about their mother, their husband, their grandmother. Sometimes it is clear to me that they are extremely frightened. And increasingly, they want to talk about what I prefer to call 'assisted death', but which is still called, wrongly in my opinion, 'assisted suicide'.

I will digress slightly at this point to talk about the baggage that words carry. Let us start with suicide. As a pallid and nervous young journalist I got to know about suicide. Oh, didn't I just. It was part of my regular tasks to sit in at the coroner's court, where I learned all the manifold ways the disturbed human brain can devise to die. High bridges and trains were, I suspect, the most traumatic instruments for all concerned, especially those who had to deal with the aftermath. Newspapers were a little more kindly in those days, and we tended not to go into too much detail, but I had to listen to it. And I remember that coroners never used the word 'insanity'. They preferred the more compassionate verdict that the subject had 'taken his life while the balance of his mind was disturbed'. There was ambivalence to the phrase, a suggestion of the winds of fate and overwhelming circumstance. No need to go into the horrible details that the coroner's officer, always a policeman, mentioned to me after the case. In fact, by now, I have reached the conclusion that a person may make a decision to die because the balance of their mind is level, realistic, pragmatic, stoic and sharp. And that is why I dislike the term 'assisted suicide' being applied to the carefully thought out and weighed up process of having one's life ended by gentle medical means.

The people who thus far have made the harrowing trip to Dignitas in Switzerland to die seemed to me to be very firm and methodical of purpose, with a clear *prima facie* case for wanting their death to be on their own terms. In short, their mind may well be in better balance than the world around them.

I'll return again to my father's request to me, that I was unable to fulfil. In the course of the past year or so I have talked amiably about the issues of assisted dying to people of all sorts, because they have broached the subject. A lot of them get nervy about the term 'assisted death' and seriously nervous about 'assisted suicide', but when I mention my father's mantra about not wishing to go on living supported by the pipes and tubes they brighten up and say, 'Oh, yes, I don't have any problem with that.' That was the problem reduced from a sterile title into the wishes of a real person in whom, perhaps, they could see themselves.

When I began to draft this speech, the so-called debate on assisted dying was like a snowball fight in the dark. Now, it seems to be occupying so much space in the media that I wonder whether it is something in the air, an idea whose time is really coming. Very recently an impassioned outburst by Martin Amis in an interview he gave to the *Sunday Times* called for euthanasia booths on every street corner. I firmly believe it was there to trap the hard-of-irony, and I note that it has done so – he was, after all, a novelist talking about a new book. Did it get publicity? It surely did. Apart from being tasteless, the idea is impractical, especially if there happens to be a photo booth next door. But his anger and grief at the way elderly relatives, friends and colleagues have died is clearly genuine and shared by a great many. The post-war generation have seen what's happened to their elders and are determined that it should not happen to them.

Even more recently, the British Social Attitude Survey found that 71 per cent of religious people and 92 per cent of non-religious people were in favour of medically

41

assisted dying for patients with incurable ill-nesses if they should request it.

Insofar as there are sides in this debate, they tend to polarize around the Dignity in Dying organization, who favour assisted death in special circumstances, and the Care Not Killing Alliance whose position, in a nutshell, appears to be that care will cope.

And once again I remember my father. He did not want to die a curious kind of living death. He wasn't that kind of person. He wanted to say goodbye to me, and, knowing him, he would probably have finished with a joke of some sort. And if the nurses had put the relevant syringe in the cannula, I would have pressed it, and felt it was my duty. There would have been tears, of course there would: tears would be appropriate and unsuppressable.

But of course, this did not happen because I, my father and the nurses were locked in the aspic of the law. But he actually had a good death in the arms of morphia and I envy him.

I got involved in the debate surrounding 'assisted death' by accident after taking a long and, yes, informed look at my future as someone with Alzheimer's and subsequently writing an article about my conclusions. As a result of my 'coming out' about the disease I now have contacts in medical research industries all over the world, and I have no reason to believe that a 'cure' is imminent. I do think, on their good advice, that there may be some very interesting developments in the next couple of years and I'm not the only one to hope for some kind of 'stepping stone' – a treatment that will keep me going long enough for a better treatment to be developed.

I said earlier that PCA at the endgame is effectively the same as Alzheimer's and that it is the most feared disease among the elderly.

I was diagnosed when I was fifty-nine, but it has struck adults in their thirties. I enjoy my life, and wish to continue it for as long as I am still myself, knowing who I am and recognizing my nearest and dearest. But I know enough about the endgame to be fearful of it, despite the fact that as a wealthy man I could probably shield myself from the worst; even the wealthy, whatever they may do, have their appointment in Samarra. For younger members of the audience, I should say that the fable 'Appointment in Samarra' is probably one of the oldest stories in the world and has been recast many times; its central point is that you can run and you can hide, but every man has his inevitable appointment with death. It's worth a Google.

Back in my early reporting days I was told something that surprised me at the time: nobody has to do what the doctor tells them. I learned this when the Chief Reporter, George

Topley, slung my copy back at me and said, 'Never say that a patient has been released from hospital unless you are talking about someone who is being detained on mental grounds. The proper word is "discharged", and even though the staff would like you to believe that you can't just walk out until they say so, you damn well can. Although, generally speaking, it's best not to be dragging a portable life-support system down the steps with you.' George was a remarkable journalist who as a fiery young man would have fought fascism in the Spanish Civil War were it not for the fact that he stowed away on the wrong boat and ended up in Hull.

And I remembered what George said and vowed that rather than let Alzheimer's take me, I would take it. I would live my life, as ever, to the full and die, before the disease mounted its last attack, in my own home, in a chair on the lawn, with a brandy in my hand to wash down whatever modern version of the 'Brompton Cocktail' (a potent mixture of painkillers and brandy) some helpful medic could supply. And with Thomas Tallis on my iPod, I would shake hands with Death.

I have made my position publicly clear; it seems to me quite a reasonable and sensible decision, for someone with a serious, incurable and debilitating disease to elect for a medically assisted death by appointment.

These days non-traumatic deaths – not the best word, but you will know what I mean – which is to say, deaths that don't, for example, involve several cars, a tanker and a patch of ice on the M4 – largely take place in hospitals and hospices. Not so long ago death took place in your own bed. The Victorians knew how to die. They saw a lot of death. And Victorian and Edwardian London was awash with what we would call recreational drugs, which were seen as a boon and a blessing to all. Departing on schedule with the help of a friendly doctor was quite usual and there is every reason to believe that the medical profession considered that part of its duty was to help the stricken patient on their way.

Does that still apply? It would seem so. Did the Victorians fear death? As Death says in one of my own books, most men don't fear death, they fear those things – the knife, the shipwreck, the illness, the bomb – which precede, by microseconds if you're lucky, and many years if you're not, the moment of death.

And this brings us into the whole care or killing argument.

The Care Not Killing Alliance, as they phrase themselves, assure us that no one need consider a voluntary death of any sort since care is always available. This is questionable. Medicine is keeping more and more people alive, all requiring more and more care.

Alzheimer's and other dementias place a huge care burden on the country, a burden which falls initially on the next of kin who may even be elderly and, indeed, be in need of some sort of care themselves. The number is climbing as the Baby Boomers get older but, in addition, the percentage of cases of dementia among the population is also growing. We then have to consider the quality of whatever care there may be, not just for dementia but for all long-term conditions. I will not go into the horror stories, this is not the place and maybe I should leave the field open to Sir Michael Parkinson who, as the government's Dignity Ambassador, describes incidents that are, and I quote, 'absolutely barmy and cruel beyond belief' and care homes as little more than 'waiting rooms for death'.

It appears that care is a lottery and there are those of us who don't wish to be cared for and who do not want to spend their time in anyone's waiting room, who want to have the right not to do what you are told by a nurse, not to obey the doctor. A right, in my case, to demand here and now the power of attorney over the fate of the Terry Pratchett that, at some future date, I will become. People exercise themselves in wondering what their nearest and dearest would really want. Well, my nearest and dearest know. So do you.

A major objection frequently flourished by opponents of 'assisted dying' is that elderly people might be illegally persuaded into 'asking' for assisted death. Could be, but the *Journal of Medical Ethics* reported in 2007 that there was no evidence of abuse of vulnerable patients in Oregon where assisted dying is currently legal. I don't see why things should be any different here. I'm sure nobody considers death flippantly; the idea that people would persuade themselves to die just because some hypothetical Acme

One-Stop Death shop has opened down the road is fantastical. But I can easily envisage that a person, elderly or otherwise, weighed down with medical problems and understandably fearful of the future, and dreading what is hopefully called care, might consider the 'Victorian-style' death, gently assisted by a medical professional, at home, a more dignified way to go.

Last year, the government finally published guidelines on dealing with assisted death. They did not appear to satisfy anybody. It seems that those wishing to assist a friend or relative to die would have to meet quite a large number of criteria in order to escape the chance of prosecution for murder. We should be thankful that some possibility that they might not be prosecuted is in theory possible, but as laid out, the best anyone can do is keep within the rules and hope for the best.

That's why I and others have suggested some kind of strictly non-aggressive tribunal that would establish the facts of the case well before the assisted death takes place. This might make some people, including me, a little uneasy as it suggests the government has the power to tell you whether you can live or die. But that said, the government cannot sidestep the responsibility to ensure the protection of the vulnerable and we must respect that. It grieves me that those against assisted death seem to assume, as a matter of course, that those of us who support it have not thought long and hard about this very issue and know that it is of fundamental importance. It is, in fact, at the soul and centre of my argument.

The members of the tribunal would be acting for the good of society as well as that of the applicant, horrible word, and ensure they are of sound and informed mind, firm in their purpose, suffering from a life-threatening and incurable disease and not under the influence of a third party. It would need wiser heads than mine, though heaven knows they should be easy enough to find, to determine how such tribunals are constituted. But I would suggest there should be a lawyer, one with expertise in dynastic family affairs who has become good at recognizing what somebody really means and, indeed, whether there is outside pressure. And a medical practitioner experienced in dealing with the complexities of serious long-term illnesses.

Those opposing 'assisted death' say that the vulnerable must be protected, as if that would not have occurred to anyone else. As a matter of fact there is no evidence – and evidence has been sought – of the sick or elderly being cajoled into assisted death by relatives anywhere in the world where assisted dying is practised, and I see no reason why that would be the case here. Doctors tell me that, to the contrary, family members more often beg them to keep Granny alive even when Granny is indeed, by all medical standards, at the end of her natural life. Importantly, the tribunal would also serve to prevent, as far as humanly possible, any abuses.

I would also suggest that all those on the tribunal are over forty-five years old, by which time they may have acquired the rare gift of wisdom, because wisdom and compassion should in this tribunal stand side by side with the law. The tribunal would also have to be a check on those seeking death for reasons that reasonable people may consider trivial or transient distress. I dare say that quite a few people have contemplated death for reasons that much later seemed to them to be quite minor. If we are to live in a world where a socially acceptable 'early death' can be allowed, it must be allowed as a result of careful consideration.

Let us consider me as a test case. As I have said, I would like to die peacefully with Thomas Tallis on my iPod before the disease takes me over and I hope that will not be for quite some time to come, because if I knew that I could die at any time I wanted, then suddenly every day would be as precious as a million pounds. If I knew that I could die, I would live. My life, my death, my choice.

There has been no evidence in those areas where assisted dying is currently practised that it leads to any kind of 'slippery slope'. It seems to be an item of faith among those opposed to assisted dying that it will open the door to abuses all the way up to the culling of the elderly sick. This is a nightmare and only a nightmare. This cannot be envisaged in any democracy unless we find ourselves under a tyranny, that is to say a tyranny that is far more aggressive than the mild one currently operated by the Health and Safety Executive. Frankly, that objection is a bogeyman.

It has been suggested that people would not trust their doctor if they knew that he or she had the power to kill them. Why should this be? A doctor has an awful lot to lose by killing a patient. Indeed, it seems to me that asking a medical practitioner who is fully aware of your situation to bring your life to an end is placing the utmost trust in them.

The saying 'Thou shalt not kill; but needst not strive officiously to keep alive' has never been formal advice to the medical profession. Given that it was made up by Arthur Hugh Clough, who was in a similar profession to me, that is not surprising. But, ever since the birth of medicine, doctors have understood its meaning. They have striven, oh how they have striven. In the past two centuries we have improved the length of our lives and the quality of said lives to the point where we feel somewhat uneasy if anyone dies as early as the biblical age of seventy. But there comes a time when technology outpaces sense, when a blip on an oscilloscope is confused with life, and humanity unravels into a state of mere existence.

Observation, conversation and some careful deduction lead me to believe that the majority of doctors who support the right to die are those who are most closely involved day to day with patients, while support appears to tail off as you reach those heights where politics and medicine merge. It would be interesting to speculate how many doctors would 'come out' were it not for the baleful glare of the BMA. Anyone who has any long-term friendships, acquaintances or professional dealings within the medical profession, let alone knows anything about the social history of medicine, knows that down the ages doctors and nurses have seen it as part of their duty to allow those beyond hope and skill to depart in peace. I can recall the metaphors that have been used: 'helping them over the step', 'showing them the way', 'helping them find the door', 'pointing them to Heaven'. But never, ever 'killing them', because in their minds they were not killing and in their minds they were right.

In fact, I have not found any reputable information from those places where assisted death is allowed that shows any deleterious effect on the community. I certainly do not expect or assume that every GP or hospital practitioner would be prepared to assist death by arrangement, even in the face of overwhelming medical evidence. That is their choice. Choice is very important in this matter. But there will be some, probably older, probably wiser, who will understand. It seems sensible to me that we should look to the medical profession, that over the centuries has helped us to live longer and healthier lives, to help us die peacefully among our loved ones in our own home without a long stay in God's waiting room.

And finally there is the God argument, which I think these days appears to have been subsumed into concern for the innocent who may suffer if assisted dying were allowed. The problem with the God argument is that it only works if you believe in God, more specifically, Jehovah, which I do not. Spinoza, Darwin and Carl Sagan have found in my imagination places which God has never found. Therefore I am a humanist and would rather believe that we are a rising ape, not a falling angel. Nevertheless, I have a sneaking regard for the Church of England and those I disagree with. We should always debate ideas that appear to strike at the centre of our humanity. Ideas and proposals should be tested. I believe that consensual 'assisted death' for those that ask for it is quite hard to oppose, especially by those that have some compassion. But we do need in this world people to remind us that we are all human, and that humanity is precious.

It's that much heralded thing, the quality of life, that is important. How you live your life, what you get out of it, what you put into it and what you leave behind after it. We should aim for a good and rich life well lived and, at the end of it, in the comfort of our own home, in the company of those who love us, have a death worth dying for.

**Terry Pratchett** was the acclaimed creator of the global bestselling Discworld series, the first of which, *The Colour of Magic*, was published in 1983. His fortieth Discworld novel, *Raising Steam*, was published in 2013. His books have been widely adapted for stage and screen, and he was the winner of multiple prizes, including the Carnegie Medal, as well as being awarded a knighthood for services to literature. He died in March 2015.

www.terrypratchett.co.uk

# BY TERRY PRATCHETT

Snuff

Raising Steam

The Shepherd's Crown (for young adults)


## NON-DISCWORLD BOOKS

The Dark Side of the Sun

Strata

The Unadulterated Cat (illustrated by Gray Jolliffe)

Good Omens (with Neil Gaiman)


## SHORTER WRITING

A Blink of the Screen

A Slip of the Keyboard


## WITH STEPHEN BAXTER

The Long Earth

The Long War

The Long Mars

The Long Utopia

## NON-DISCWORLD BOOKS FOR YOUNG ADULTS

A complete list of Terry Pratchett ebooks and audio books as well as other books based on the Discworld series – illustrated screenplays, graphic novels, comics and plays – can be found on www.terrypratchett.co.uk